Listening
to the
Garden
Grow

Listening to the Garden Grow

❧

Finding Miracles in Daily Life

Betty Sue Eaton

✻ STILLPOINT PUBLISHING

☀ STILLPOINT PUBLISHING

*Books to awaken the human spirit and build a society
that honors the Earth, Humanity, and The Sacred in All Life.*

This book is manufactured in the United States of America.
Cover and interior artwork designed by Karen Savary.

Published by Stillpoint Publishing, Box 640,
Meetinghouse Road, Walpole, NH 03608

ISBN: 1-883478-14-6

Dedication

For Grover, Pam, Richard and Paula, with love

Contents

Acknowledgements

There are several people whom I wish to thank for directly or indirectly helping me to write *Listening to the Garden Grow*. The first one is my husband, Grover, without whose help, encouragement and support, I could never have had my garden. I could not forget my father, Travis Barrett Hicks, for teaching me to appreciate things growing. Another is my friend, Dorothy Wilcox, who is no longer with us, for her deep appreciation of the beauty and messages from my garden. My friend and mentor, Linn Mills, Horticulturist for the Clark County office of the U.S. Department of Agriculture Extension Service, has helped me to show people in Las Vegas, Nevada, U.S.A., what can be done in a backyard vegetable garden in a very hostile natural environment. For all that, I am deeply appreciative. To Wanda Falls, Nono

Burkhart, Barbara and Walt Horlyck, Pam Kirk, and Marilynn Landreth for encouraging me to publish my thoughts to share with others.

A special thanks to Meredith Young-Sowers and Claire Gerus at Stillpoint Publishing, who have given me this wonderful opportunity to share my love of gardening and Nature with my readers.

Foreword

They say in the East (by East I mean Japan, Thailand, and Vietnam—not Massachusetts and Connecticut!) that we are born with *bijas,* or dream seeds, in our soul.

Each of us has the choice to water these seeds with mindful awareness, to provide a nurturing environment in which they can grow straight and tall, as sunflowers do, reaching toward the light. What comes to us then as seed will be passed on to another as blossom, and what comes to us as blossom, will be passed on to another as fruit.

Several years ago, one March day, I was in Rhode Island walking along a gravel road that led to the ocean. A very old and very thin woman came hobbling down a driveway towards me. I waved and continued walking, but as I passed, she grabbed my arm, turned around and began to pull me in

11

the direction of her house. I instantly thought of the witch in *Hansel and Gretel*, and tried to pull back, but that only made her clutch my wrist more tightly. Besides, she didn't cackle, so I relented.

She didn't say a word, in fact, until we approached her house. It was a shingle-style cottage with green shutters and a front lawn erupting everywhere in purple crocuses. She released me there, throwing her arms up in the air and shouting, "Look at this splendor! Isn't it a miracle?!"

I didn't know what to say. I mean, the crocuses were everywhere and indeed they were beautiful, but a miracle? Besides, I had been thinking about a very important problem when she had interrupted me and...

I was snapped out of my reverie as the old woman threw her arms around me. She whispered in my ear, "You don't understand. As you grow a garden, it grows you!"

The woman, I later learned, was Betts Wodehouse. After that, I visited her every chance I could. It turned out she was a famous sculptress whose mother had been friends with August Rodin.

I never went inside Betts' house. We always went directly to her garden. At age ninety or so, it was hard for her to bend down and weed, so I'd do it for her. One day, she talked on and on about a particular weed that had spread everywhere and couldn't be pulled out without taking some of the healthy plants. I realized later she was also telling me that she had incurable cancer.

Each time we were together, she taught me about gardening. But when I arrived home, I knew she had been offering me lessons of the soul, as well, lessons to nourish my dream seeds. As I would walk away down the gravel driveway, she'd always call to me, "Don't forget, as you grow your garden, your garden grows you!"

When I first picked up Betty Sue Eaton's little book, *Listening to the Garden Grow: Finding Miracles in Daily Life,* it was as if Betts had grabbed my wrist all over again, showing me another woman who had been "grown" by her garden. I knew it was another "random act of kindness, a senseless gift of beauty." I read it slowly, as if I were perusing the secret journal of a woman learning to nurture the seeds in her soul so the strong winds of time could blow them onto those of us who so dearly need to be reminded to stay true to our deepest longings.

May the seeds that blow from these pages to you root deeply in the rich soil of your heart and mind.

Dawna Markova, Ph.D.
Vermont, 1996

Preface

I do many things to keep my mind off events over which I have no control. I weave, paint, craft stained glass, and enjoy several other hobbies. But the most rewarding thing I do is garden. I love working in my garden because I know that my family, friends, and neighbors will benefit from my efforts to produce bounty from the soil.

And I have found another benefit from tending the garden: I have discovered my own special place to be still and to regenerate.

Today, as every day, I enjoy my early morning meditation on the patio facing my plants. These morning communions lift my spirits and help me face whatever the day may bring.

I believe that if we have faith that God creates all things, we are ultimately brought into harmony with the

Creator's Will. One reason I so enjoy having a garden is that I can watch God's miracles at work daily. By taking these miracles to a higher level, I can believe that God works miracles in me and in my life, as well. After all, how much closer are human beings to God's image, than plants.

But without a doubt, the overriding reason for this small book is to express to readers my belief that, even in the face of great adversity and heartache, there is a quiet place to go to meditate, to believe in God's blessings, and to be so quiet within, they can almost hear the garden grow.

In my experience, the greatest gift we can offer is the gift of sharing. And so, just as God shares the peace and bounty of my garden with me and my loved ones, I wish to extend my experiences in this sacred place to my readers. I hope that everyone who shares these reflections will realize that a loving connection with the Creator is not only possible, but inevitable, here in the garden of Life.

Betty Sue Eaton
Nevada, 1996

Whose Garden is This?

My garden is a restful place
Where all my tensions leave,
Its scented quiet soothes my face
And pleasure tugs my sleeve.

I planted tiny seeds in spring
their bounty locked inside,
And waited for the rain to bring
Their miracle alive.

I worked the soil and waited then,
Not patiently, at best,
I watered, fed, and pinched and thinned,
Sat back and took a rest.

But I can't take the praise for Life,
I only gave a prayer
That lush and tender things would grow,
For God was working there.

Planting
the
Seeds

Bless this Soil

Dear Lord,

Bless this soil in my garden, that it may be productive.
Bless the working of Thy Holy Hands, which shaped the mountains from whence it came.
Bless the ancients whose feet left prints in eons past, now blown away and forgotten.
Bless the animals that fed on meager, life-sustaining plants given by the sun and rain.
Bless the bones of ancients and animals that enriched the soil in my garden.
Bless the soil in my garden, that it may be productive.
Bless me, Oh Lord, that I may do honor to it.

Thank You, Lord.

Amen.

21

Planting Memories

I think I'll plant a memory today. I never really thought of my garden as anything other than a source of wonderful fruits and vegetables. But today I realized that I have always planted things that surrounded me while growing up. These plants have come to mean home, family, and love to me. So today, I think I'll go out and plant another special memory!

When I was a child of ten or eleven, my grandparents lived across the orchard from us in a small wooden house. There was a path, of course, between their place and ours. Along the path, Dad had planted giant sunflowers. When they were all grown, they stood eight or nine feet high, far above the reach of my younger brother and sister and me. We longed to reach the fat seeds in the dinner-plate-sized heads, but only the birds could do that.

As the monstrous flowers aged, their heads would turn down to face us as we scurried up and down the trail to Grandmother's house, but still we couldn't reach them. It was simply out of the question that we should pull one over and cut off a gigantic head.

One hot summer day, we three chilren were playing in the ditch that separated our orchard from Granddad's garden. As the humid day wore on into still, sticky afternoon, sounds of thunder began. We could hear Mother calling us to come inside quickly, for there was sure to be hail and high winds with the clouds about to break over us.

Like most children, we were reluctant to leave our fantasy world for the real one. Mother called again and again, more urgently. Finally, we felt the first drops of cold rain and the sudden gust of wind on our faces. As we ran for the path toward the house, the wind gusted even stronger and rain and hail pelted us, stinging our faces, backs, and arms. The wind seemed to be in charge as we ran. With every third or so step of ours, it would pick us up off the ground, our small legs churning in the air, putting us at the level of the violently shaking sunflower heads.

Finally, we reached the back door and fell inside, three drained, drenched "young'uns," as Granddad called us. Thunder boomed constantly; lightning flashed every second, and the wind howled, puffing the doors in and out like the wolf in *The Three Little Pigs*. Gradually, the storm

abated and everything was cool, freshly washed, and spanking clean.

And speaking of spanking, we came very close to getting one. It turned out that the "storm" was a small tornado hop-skipping up to where our house was sitting. In fact, every spring, at least one of our farm buildings was taken by a tornado. Dad used to complain that we had the newest out-buildings in the county—every year!

So today, I am going to plant a sunflower memory. The sight of those dinner-plate-sized heads turning their faces down to mine will remind me of the days when I was a child, living in the borderland between fantasy and reality, securely wrapped in the warmth of my family's love, and awed by the sight of those huge golden faces.

Seed Packets

It is always exciting to sit down and make out my spring seed order. As I pore over the bright pages of the catalog, I can almost taste the luscious fruits and vegetables pictured there in glorious color. Then, with pen in hand, I plan my garden work for the next year, post my order, and sit back to await the coming of my seed packets.

On the day my order arrives, I go through the packets, picturing where the contents of each will be planted in my garden. I am always amazed that the contents of these small, flat seed packets, once matured, will produce jars and jars of tomato sauce, pickles, kraut, beets and other delights. I look at the packet of corn seed and can almost taste the sweet, buttery kernels retrieved from the stacks of corn in my freezer. I can just smell the spicy, vinegary odors filling my

kitchen as I pack away young cucumbers for curing into sweet pickles. Then, I am reminded of other delights stored in other kinds of packets.

There are so many treasures that have been grown from "seed packets of the heart"—loving gifts we offer each other. These may be a reassuring smile for a stranger in a hospital hallway, or a small, homemade bouquet taken to an ill neighbor.

I am constantly touched by the seeds of love and understanding I receive from others. My husband's obvious love and care are tucked away in my heart's seed packet and nurtured daily. And, when a friend and fellow instructor learned of a tragic illness in my family and gave me a heartfelt hug of understanding, I gratefully added his seeds of empathy to the other treasures in my heart's seed packet.

I also store with great tenderness the joy on the faces of young nieces and nephews when I arrive for a visit. And when I receive a phone call from a lifelong friend after a year's silence, I know that she still has me in her heart, and that I will always be there.

These little "seed treasures" are endless—I only need remember that they are there. Unlike Burpee's seed packets, the one that contains my heart's treasures is infinite in size, its stored memories protected by the One Who creates all things. And accompanying this gift is the privilege of receiving these seeds of love, to treasure always.

The next time my spring seeds arrive, I will remember that I exchange a more precious variety of "seeds" every day with people I love. These will never go out of date, never be damaged, never be ruined or lost. They are God's gifts to me and mine, to cherish and nurture us more completely than the contents of any commercial seed packet could ever do.

Spring Magic

Although spring approaches, today is miserable, with a raw, cold, blustery wind chilling me to the bone. How can I be thankful for a day such as this? Not easily, I admit.

Yet Nature has a surprise for me, and as I look out my window, I see that magic is once again at work in my garden. Several robins are grazing among the iris shoots. But upon closer examination, I see perhaps forty or fifty other birds excitedly extracting worms from the back lawn. Moving to the sliding glass doors for a better look, I'm aware of another flutter, and suddenly swarms of the red-breasted birds are blanketing my entire garden and orchard.

Fascinated, I step out onto the patio and marvel at the sight of the undulating red and gray sheet in my backyard. All at once, a crash of thunder and a sudden gust of wind

28

cause the birds to erupt into flight. How disappointed I am to see them go. But Nature again surprises me. After circling around for a few minutes, the robins descend once more into my garden and hungrily return to their repast of worms and other insects brought up for air by the rain.

Now, hundreds of robins line the ridge and eaves of the roof, the top of the back fence, the pyracantha bush on the front fence, and even the cab of the pickup truck just off the patio. I am totally awestruck!

The robins' arrival has offered me a respite of sheer, unadulterated joy. This has been an afternoon the likes of which I have never seen.

Yes, the day opened dismal and gray. But the robins' visit—like a delightful drop-in from friends—has changed everything.

Today has reminded me that each of us is blessed with "robins" that come to brighten our days—even when Life seems most dreary. I will always remember the day when the red-feathered variety visited my world and lifted my spirits on their gentle wings.

Harbingers

The vacant garden slumbers under the cold winds of winter after a rich, bountiful summer. It waits, even as I do, for the awakening of spring. But even in its slumber, it is not idle. The garden provides all manner of feasts for feathered travelers passing our way on their flight to warmer climes.

On several mornings when I look outside, I see hundreds of doves grazing on seeds left after the harvest. As Di, our miniature poodle, charges at the invaders, whistling wings explode into the air, only to circle and return to their repast when Di has retreated to the warmth of the house.

Wrens, sparrows, finches, meadowlarks, and robins have all enjoyed our garden as we wait for spring to return. And that event is imminent—the pair of kestrals that migrated elsewhere are back, searching the neighborhood

30

backyards and gardens for field mice, voles, lizards and chipmunks for their meals. They sit on the light pole and chatter amongst themselves, causing Di to cast a wary eye and wonder what manner of creature they are.

Our fruit trees are adorned with the budding forerunners of the blooms they will sport. Not having observed the apple trees since we sprayed them over a month ago, I am surprised to see new, greening twigs at the ends of barren branches. Daffodils are pushing their dark green leaves from their cold bed, serving notice that soon a dazzling display of yellow blossoms will salute the Heritage Oak tree under which they lie. Everything is stirring in my garden, and it doesn't stop there!

I feel a stirring in me as well—to once again return to the soil that I love, and to stir it once more into another summer harvest of rich produce and beauty. The voice of Nature that calls my garden into being calls me as well, and I welcome the opportunity to blend my energy with that of my seedlings. The harbingers of spring invite me to join them, and I willingly respond—eager to help create new miracles in my garden.

An Optimist's Garden

Down in the deep South, where there is lush green vegetation and plenty of moisture, gardening is expected to be easy. But in the high sterile desert area of Las Vegas, Nevada, gardening is not expected at all!

A few years ago, when we arrived in Nevada, I found it difficult to find employment. Guilt-driven to be busy and productive, I urged my long-suffering husband to let me have a backyard garden. He agreed, saying that if I was willing to dig up the virgin lawn where I wanted this little corner of Paradise, he would install a sprinkler system.

Although philosophically opposed to tough labor, I recognized that there had to be an initial period of sheer hard work to get the project ready. So I accepted the inevitable, and began.

First, I stepped off the area of the lawn to be removed, went to the garage for the pick and shovel, and dug in—literally! By evening, I had removed a strip of lawn eight by ten feet along one end of the yard. My husband, Grover, somewhat surprised by my industry, joined in. It took me three weeks to dig out some 450 square feet of virgin lawn around one corner of the backyard. What remained was a huge, ugly cavity six inches deep, with clumps of grass heaped in the middle of the remaining lawn. That was not a pretty picture, and neither were my hands!

Grover and I spent another two weeks sifting dirt out of the clumps and spading it back into the garden, disposing of the excess grass. We edged the area with railroad cross ties, bedding them in the bottom of the cavity. The edge followed the pattern of the corner eight feet out, which is the length of one cross tie. This gave our soon-to-be-green farmland visible boundaries to keep the soil in and the lawn grass out.

Then, we laid out the sprinkler system with heads at ground level, allowing for twelve inches of topsoil. We ordered ten cubic yards of soil, which we wheelbarrowed to the backyard. Finally, we leveled it, looked at it, and said, "It is good."

Ever the optimist, I planted many varieties of seeds and bedding plants until every last foot of soil was filled. We also planted nectarine, peach and apricot trees, which we

spaced evenly at each end and in the middle of the garden. To our delight, they flourished. I was pleased to find that the close planting of seeds made weeding nonexistent. The ground stayed moist and cool, promising signs for good, healthy future plants.

However, I did lose my entire crop of green beans to a sticky, honeylike substance from whiteflies. One day, when I wore a yellow tee shirt into the garden, whiteflies literally turned it white as they swarmed over me. They apparently have an affinity for yellow. I considered how I might use this to my advantage in future planting endeavors!

Undaunted, I continued to learn lessons from my garden. As the years went by, I became selective in my choice of seeds but still used the close planting technique which had proven to be very water-efficient and productive. I remembered what my Dad had done on the farm to insure continuing soil vigor, and I rotated my crops so as not to plant the same thing in the same place two years in a row. It worked beautifully!

Grover and I are now in the fifth year of our garden, and are anticipating the usual abundance. We have joyfully identified the crops that we like best, and that yield the most. We have doubled our usual number of broccoli, cauliflower, Brussels sprouts and cabbage from six each to twelve. We also have sweet peas, bell peppers, cherry and standard tomatoes, zucchini and butternut squash, cantaloupes, watermelon, eggplant, cucumbers, cherry and chili peppers, radishes, strawberries, garlic, chives, turnips, asparagus, and black-eyed peas. In a gun crate converted to a planter, we have dill, oregano, summer savory, sage, basil and rosemary.

I now spend no more than 10 to 15 minutes a day working in the garden, and most of that time is spent looking in wonder at what can be done in an optimist's high desert garden.

It is an endless source of satisfaction for the whole family, and I still have time for my loved ones. I can't, however, take all of the credit; my husband runs the heavy rototiller to prepare the soil for spring planting and my Dad educated me in the ways of growing things. But my most important team member is God, probably grinning broadly at the efforts of this optimistic lady gardener who keeps trying to create a new kind of beauty in a place where one would least expect it. Creating beauty from nothing is hardly a new idea, however; doesn't our Creator do that all the time?

Life's Wonderful Accidents

Why is it that the tomato seed from a discarded plant, dropped in the most unexpected place, is the one that outdoes itself? And why is it that the seeds you placed very carefully at precise intervals in neat little rows often refuse to grow in regimented lock step?

I don't know why, but I do know this: some of the most rewarding friendships begin by accident. Take, for instance, the young man at the neighborhood nursery. I was tracking down some pistachio trees when I met him. He had no trees, but we continued to talk and soon discovered a mutual passion for irises. Now, we swap stories and plant specimens, to our mutual delight.

Here's another example: Helen, my 82-year-old neighbor down the street, entered our lives years ago when we moved into the neighborhood. The town paper had written a feature about our garden, and she stopped by to show me the newspaper clipping.

Later, I brought her some fresh spinach, and invited her to visit the now-famous (at least locally) garden. Since then, in addition to a passion for flowers, we have discovered a mutual love of writing and reading.

Last fall, I brought Helen a Halloween bouquet. I took a small pumpkin from the garden, hollowed it out, and filled it to overflowing with button mums, finishing it off with carrot tops for greenery. I told Helen that, after she had enjoyed the flowers, she could eat the vase. She loved the idea, and did, in fact, make pumpkin pie!

Since then, when Helen feels low, she devises a reason to come to my house. As we sit on the patio overlooking my garden, we might talk, or simply sit in friendly silence. The look on her face tells me that the visit was worth more than any amount of time she could have spent in a therapist's office.

I could go on with these "accidental" friendships, but the point is this: I now know that, whatever happens in a day, a week, or a month, if I can accept Life's gifts whenever or wherever they occur, I will be richly rewarded.

Apparently, people, as well as plants, tend to thrive when spontaneity is a part of their lives.

Nurturing the Seedlings

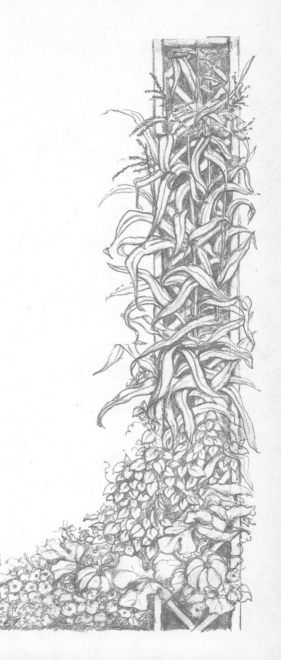

The Lesson of the Corn

Dear Lord,

Today, I was so troubled with the noise in my life. I was even more troubled when I saw that my beautiful corn had fallen down in a storm last night. Futilely, I tried to brace it up, but each time I tried, it fell again.

In despair I retreated, leaving the corn to its end: the compost bin. But then, when I looked at the stalks the next morning, the tips were turning up to the light.

Your lesson was not lost on me: If, when storms whirl around me, I reach for the Light, You will lift me up, as You did the tips of the corn, just as You promised.

Thank You, Lord.

Amen.

41

Provisions at a Price

Some people might wonder why I prefer to punish my back, stooping over rows of peas in the heat rather than attacking my housecleaning. They might also wonder why I prefer to work up a mighty sweat, rather than write my school lesson plans in the cool, pleasant study. Both of these inside chores provide me with satisfaction, but they do not enrich my soul.

Gardening, on the other hand, is a source of deep pleasure. I never tire of watching each season's crops grow through their stages, or observing the birds and insects which thrive there. My garden is indeed the site of wondrous activities, and I love being its caretaker. But I must admit, the provisions from my garden come at a price.

On steaming summer days, I struggle with heat and back pain after hours of bending and stooping over my plants. Rivulets of sweat run down my face, dropping onto my glasses and into my eyes so I can't see. Sugar ants bite my ankles, and the okra leaves irritate my arms until I scratch them raw. And I've been known to have encounters with bumble bees and wasps when I invade their territory so I can gather vegetables from among the blossoms on which they feed.

I must admit, too, that after all my hard work, I'm horrified when I reach for a cluster of black-eyed peas and find that mice have already chewed the peas out of the pods, leaving the shells hanging empty. And I "see red" when I search the vines for a newly ripened cantaloupe and disturb the zillion whiteflies feasting on the leaves.

Why do I subject myself to this misery? Because I consider all these discomforts a small price to pay for the joy of producing fresh, healthy food for my loved ones. When beaming smiles and warm compliments surround me at harvest time, I am filled with pleasure that the fruits (and vegetables) of my labors have been lovingly grown and received. And I give thanks to the Creator for showing me how I can provide for others.

For me, gardening—despite the stiff joints and occasional nips from insects—is far more than an experience of work; in many ways, it is an experience of worship.

Preferred Priorities

Once again, the floor needs sweeping; I can write my name in the dust near the kitchen door. But first, I have to go see how the cilantro is progressing. I may have to pinch off blooms so it will keep on growing. Then I might have to check the climbing roses for aphids on all that new growth. The yellow blooms interspersed with the red ones are so lovely that I must at least admire them on so lovely a morning.

The furniture could certainly use a good polishing. But I'm sure the strawberry blooms that I saw yesterday are about ready to set fruit, and I wouldn't want to miss that. Besides, the hybrid lilies are so beautiful, with their star-shaped faces of golden yellow, pale peach, and smoky lavender; I must talk to them and tell them how very striking they are.

44

And yes, the bills must be paid today. Reluctantly, I pull myself up to the breakfast bar and try to concentrate on this mundane chore. But it's difficult, and I find that my glance keeps straying to the panorama outside the sliding glass doors.

How can I ignore the hummers feeding voraciously at the nectar hung above the open sliding doors? They might need me to encourage them, or to break up a territorial squabble.

Then, who knows? I might have to walk around the postage-stamp-sized orchard to check the ripening of apricots, or the swelling of apples. On the other hand, I may have to pick those boysenberries hanging through the squares of fencing wire. The beans must be checked frequently to be sure they're still eating size. And one thing any zucchini grower knows is that these prolific little beauties must be watched continuously, or they will quickly grow into giant green logs.

Although it may take me a bit longer to do my accounts, it's obvious why I must do them at the breakfast bar. Here, I can watch four-foot-tall glads tugging at their stakes, shaking their long necks in the wind. I can marvel at their incredible pinks, bright oranges, lime greens, and delicate orchids. Today, the dahlias are turning their glorious faces to the sun, and accenting all this wonder is the intoxicating perfume of my Double Delight roses.

This leads me to one conclusion: tedious, boring jobs like bill-paying will never, alas, disappear. But combining these less appealing chores with a more pleasant activity, such as garden-watching, can restore pleasure to the moment. After all, isn't the quality of our time more important than the speed with which we achieve our objectives? As I gaze outdoors at my garden, I think I know the answer.

Special Benefactors

One fine spring morning, I observed a bird I had never seen before, swooping and diving into and out of the neighboring yards. I was at a loss to identify the reddish-brown, stocky little body with its rather long, finely pointed tail. Its head was blunt with a short, hooked beak and the stranger also had curved talons similar to those of the red hawk.

I had begun taking my ironing to a woman who did laundry. Because of my teaching schedule, I was too busy to do it myself. The woman's husband was a wood carver with a special interest in raptors, or birds of prey. He told me that my suspicions had been correct: my new neighborhood friend was a kestral, a species of hawk.

My garden had other new occupants, as well. I observed that my tender cabbage and broccoli plants were being enjoyed by a family of chipmunks. Later in the spring, other rodents had their way with the young corn, leaving great blocks of stubs instead of strapping stalks.

I had worked at ridding my garden of all these pests, but my battle seemed lost from the beginning. Needless to say, I was not an admirer of little varmints.

Then, the kestrals arrived on the scene! On one particularly balmy day, I watched Nature in action. There, on my neighbor's outdoor satellite dish antenna, sat two kestrals in the throes of courtship. First, the male would fly up a few feet to land near the female and nibble tenderly around her head. Then he would fly off, making forays through the yards as if searching for food. This activity continued for most of the morning.

When the male finally returned to his mate, he had a mouse in his beak, which he proceeded to feed to her. When she was finished, the happy pair flew off to their nest in a neighboring cottonwood tree.

All summer long, I observed the pair as they mated, nested, fledged chicks and then departed for the winter. I also noticed two gratifying changes in the garden: I was no longer picking empty black-eyed pea shells, and the fall crop of cabbage, broccoli and corn was flourishing. Not a single leaf had been lost to the rodent raiders.

The kestrals, who now return every year, have helped me keep my garden almost free of enterprising mice and chipmunks. How thankful I am for their presence, and for the constant reminder the Nature provides her own perfect set of checks and balances.

Both in and out of my garden, I observe in wonderment the acting out of God's plan. I see how all living things are given room to survive and nourish their mates and offspring, and then, to provide nourishment for some other form of Divinity when it is time for them to pass on.

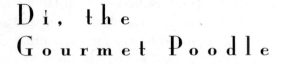

Di, the
Gourmet Poodle

Gardens are a blessing for all manner of creatures, not the least of which is me. It goes without saying that birds find them a source of food, water, and just scratching for fun, or so it seems. But an unexpected partaker of my garden's bounty is our family pet, Di, a miniature poodle.

One of the first things we noticed about her after we brought her home from the kennel was a special affinity for things growing. Then, we noticed that something was digging and eating our newly planted lima bean seeds. There were little dips in the soil just as regularly spaced as the beans I had just put there. When no sprouts emerged, I began to investigate and found absolutely no bean seeds! We further deduced one evening where the beans had gone by the size of Di's distended abdomen and the malodorous air around her.

We later observed her enthusiasm for sweet peas. When they bloomed and those little sweet green jewels began to emerge, I noticed evidence on the lawn that something was taking its liberty with my pea vines. I watched one morning as my neighbor picked a sackful of peas; there was Di, picking along beside him. "She really gets after those peas, doesn't she!" my neighbor said with amusement. But Di wasn't at all careful to just take the peas; the whole stalk followed, along with the pea pods! That's when this little veggie thief learned, "OUT, DI...OUT!"

There was further evidence of her tastes when, as a growing pup, she would go out and select only pink or red tomatoes, bring them into the kitchen, and consume them down to the blossom button on the end. First, she would nip a hole in the side of the fruit, then carefully lick out the liquid contents; then slowly, as if savoring each tasty morsel, she would nip the flesh until it was all gone. Then, almost catlike, she would clean her forelegs and paws, still relishing the taste.

All of this training as a gourmet occurred in a small backyard garden. It prepared her for serious "gourmetry" once we moved into the expanded gardening of 4500 square feet. We not only increased the size of the garden, but included corn in its variety.

Of course, the tomatoes and sweet peas were in jeopardy from day one; but to our surprise, so were many more of our prized goodies. Di has dug carrots—when I was not at home. She has invaded the green beans and left her mark as a gaping hole in the row where the beanstalks were flattened. She has tried to dig potatoes, but gave it up as a fruitless task evidenced by several small holes at the base of their green tops. I have found numerous baby green cantaloupes scattered in her "eating corner" of the backyard, so I guess they were not all that tasty. She has tried zucchini and probably found them too tough to remove from the vines. (Her teeth marks on them were visible to even the near-blind). Green peppers grow on very brittle stalks, and attached to each pepper Di took, was a goodly portion of the parent plant. Black-eyed peas were a particular favorite of hers, and she still avails herself of every opportunity to liberally sample them. She could expertly split the hull with her front teeth and delicately lift out every single pea. And then, on to bigger and better stuff!

You can imagine my surprise one day as I was sitting on our patio admiring our harvest when Di decided to pick her own ear of corn. I observed a cornstalk shaking violently. Chipmunks are nasty little thieves, but surely, I thought, they can't shake a cornstalk like that! I continued to ponder what kind of invader it could be, when out came Di, an unshucked ear of corn clenched between her teeth with the rest of the tall stalk trailing behind her. She proceeded to her "eating corner" where she expertly shucked the ear and gingerly nipped each kernel from the cob. I was so amazed that she actually picked it that I forgot to scold her!

Di has now developed an insatiable appetite for the golden morsels. Since then, we have taken the spent stalks with a few worm-eaten ears intact to the compost heap. Then, we forgot them, until we saw her making regular forays to her private larder for more of the delicious snacks. The pile of cleaned corn cobs grows larger every day.

One day, I expect to arrive home from work to find Di out in the middle of the garden, tossing a dinner salad of tomatoes, green beans, sweet peppers, maybe a little zucchini, and a couple of baby cantaloupes, topping it off with a sweet selection of golden corn on the cob. I do have to admit, she has great taste in vegetables!

Persistence

The day began with deceptive serenity. Grover had departed for work, and I sat at the breakfast bar with the patio doors open to the morning freshness. I gratefully breathed in the fragrances around me. Rich coffee aromas hung heavy on the damp air. The green shoots in the garden were still laden with raindrops; the bees were working extra hard to collect the abundant nectar from the beans, peas, squash, okra, and melon blooms; the mockingbirds, sparrows, wrens and humming-birds were squabbling for first rights to anything available.

But the morning's tranquility was shattered by angry squawks emanating from my garden. As I craned my neck to discover what was brewing, I saw a pitched battle underway between a tiny hummingbird and a newcomer challenging his territory. I watched the hummer noisily circling his rival,

54

curious as to what had his ire up. At first, I thought it must be a conflict with another hummer; they challenge each other all the time. But this time, it turned out to be a much larger opponent: it was a mockingbird!

Back and forth the little bird charged, aiming at the intruder's head and screeching his disapproval. Finally, unable to tolerate the onslaught any longer, the mockingbird burst out of the corn tassels and took refuge in the apricot tree. Still, the tiny hummingbird circled around and around until the beseiged mockingbird gave up completely and flew out of the yard.

"Good for you!" I applauded the hummer, impressed with his courage. I was reminded how often I feel threatened by problems that appear too big for me to handle. But unlike the hummingbird, I sometimes take a less assertive stance, hoping the problem will simply go away without any action on my part.

If I were to follow the lead of the spunky little hummingbird, I might actually win some of the "impossible" battles that loom before me. The hummingbird's victory proved to me that persistence, in the face of "impossible" odds, really can pay off!

Poor Man's Orchids

I grew up on a West Texas dry land farm, and when I say dry land, I mean really dry! We took our moisture when Providence deemed it was our lot, and gave thanks for it. Our natural well water supply was so laced with sodium that it collected on the pipes coming from the well, looking for all the world like a thick green collar around the metal neck where water discharged into tanks. Anything we tried to irrigate suffered an early demise. Needless to say, flower gardens were out of the question.

But I had always longed for a front yard garden, lush and dense with flowers of any kind. When I first visited Pat, my mother-in-law, I was amazed at the variety of irises that she had growing in her garden. She was a true master of the art, and her irises were glorious!

She gave me a few tubers, which I brought back to Las Vegas and planted, waiting most impatiently for them to bloom the following spring. They were magnificent, and multiplied as irises will do. When we bought the one-half acre and moved into our present home, I vowed to have an even larger iris bed.

After shopping the local iris sales, my initial bed held fifty-nine varieties planted in a small diamond-shaped plot just off our patio. How I admired them! They looked exactly like orchids.

We increased the small original bed to a fifteen-by-fifteen-foot rectangular bed and replanted all the irises, which by this time had multiplied again. They were glorious that spring, and still they continued to spread. The fourth year they were in my garden, I knew I was out of space. And when a friend in Texas sent me thirteen brand new hybrid releases, I knew I was in trouble.

Grover came up with the solution: place an ad in the paper to sell off my surplus. I did, and the venture was a success, bringing me new friends who felt exactly as I did about this "Poor Man's Orchid."

One couple, on their way from St. George, Utah, to Quartzite, Arizona, read my iris ad in the local paper and called me on their mobile phone to reserve some. Another couple, recently retired from Aramco in Saudi Arabia and establishing a new home in Las Vegas, came by and bought a

large quantity. They said they were tired of their barren landscape and wanted to fill their vistas with the rich, vibrant colors of irises. Still another immigrant couple, who could barely speak English, told me that they were not familiar with irises but would take anything that would be easy to grow in our very hot, dry climate.

Although the sale was successful, my original problem remained: I still didn't have enough space for the irises I had left. So my husband offered me a triangular strip from the end of the back lawn, vowing that this would be the last of the iris bed expansion. I now had a flower garden eighteen feet across the front end, tapering back twenty-five feet where the bed ended in almost a point. I was a very happy gardener!

Three years later, I still get phone calls from that single classified ad I placed. People delight in telling me of their own irises' beauty. They want to know if I have dug mine yet, and if I'll have any for sale this year. Most say they will buy as many of the plants as I care to sell.

What an unexpected gift that ad brought me—new friends, an opportunity to share with fellow admirers of this stately flower, and a way to pay tribute to Pat, my mentor. Although she has passed away, I often feel her presence when I'm working in the iris bed, tending with pride our "Poor Man's Orchids."

Compost Treasures

One Saturday afternoon in late spring, my husband and I were digging material from the center of the compost pile. I was trying to remove the grass from the top with a pitchfork by digging in and pulling it out to the front of the bin.

At one point, as I pulled the loaded fork away, a shower of small birds' eggs came down. With a cry of dismay, I stopped immediately. The loosened grass fell into the cavity we had created, and I quickly moved to retrieve the displaced treasures.

"You might as well discard them," Grover informed me. "Once a mother bird's nest is disturbed, she'll never return to it."

But I just couldn't toss away the nineteen blue-and-brown speckled eggs. We had no idea what kind of bird had

chosen to lay her eggs in the small, down-lined nest atop the dried grass in the compost bin. Mockingbirds galore parade around our yard; a pair of kestrals wheel in and out of the neighborhood yards foraging for rodents, lizards and anything else they can find. And on a few special occasions, a pair of Gambel's quail have grazed across the orchard and garden, using our block fence as a trail.

After restoring the nest to the top of the compost heap, I reshaped it, replaced the eggs, and prayed that I hadn't destroyed the brood. Next morning, as I left for my teaching job, I checked the nest site. The eggs were stone cold. Upon arriving home that evening, I checked again. I touched the eggs, but there was still no evidence of a mother bird's warmth.

Grover gently tried to tell me that the bird would never return. But when I went to check the next morning, I couldn't believe my eyes. There, peeking above the rim of dried grass on the compost heap, was the small, proud head of a Gambel's quail hen! She sat absolutely still, and I envisioned her one day leading a queue of tiny chicks along my fence, just as I had seen as a youngster on our farm.

Upon returning from work that afternoon, I checked again, and there she sat. "Thank you, God," I breathed.

For a third morning, I found her on her nest. But when I returned that afternoon, the eggs had been destroyed. A predator had eaten or ruined all of them. I could have cried with disappointment.

The quail couple disappeared after that, and I busied myself with other activities. But I never forgot the sight of those ruined quail eggs. I was still heartbroken by the loss of that potential addition to our family.

A few weeks later, I was resting on the patio when the quail couple appeared, foraging among the lima bean vines. They ambled around the garden, then scratched out beds in the cool, damp soil. Later, after their siesta, they rose and majestically exited my yard.

I was ecstatic! Perhaps some day, I speculated, when I least expect it, I might discover yet another unexpected cache of lovely specked quail eggs.

The silver lining behind the tragedy of the quail eggs was not lost on me. Often, when Life seems to close a door, another will open. I must always remember that God knows what I need, and why, and when. Then, I can accept a Greater Will more easily—and get ready for the next miracle.

Storms in the Corn

The corn is quiet now. Yesterday and for several days before, the wind tossed and tangled it, the tasseled heads and silken arms flailing the air. The tassels were waving about like a child caught up in a nightmare, unable to shake free from it.

Sometimes, I feel like the corn in my field, flailing the air during a storm and praying I'll survive the turmoil of the wind and rain.

We human beings encounter "storms in the corn" in many forms: a lost job, a chronic substance abuse habit, a serious illness. . . .Whatever the challenge, most of us react similarly when faced with one of Life's storms. First comes shock, then dismay, then anger, frustration, and depression. But these responses to "bad weather" may be far less effective than the example set by the corn in my garden.

The rain, hail and wind may blow fiercely, twisting the tender corn plants until they almost snap. But when all is quiet, they immediately begin to reach for the light, taking strength from even the palest of rays. Once again, the plants begin to align themselves with the Almighty, Who gives them strength to survive, even in the most hostile environments.

A garden is God's gift—a metaphor for Life. All elements there support and intertwine with each other. If I can raise myself up to reach the Light during my own storms, I am sure to receive as much healing as the occupants of my garden.

Harvesting the Crop

Sharing the Bounty

Dear Lord,

Help me to be ever mindful of the many ways to share.
Whether I am sharing flowers, or vegetables from my garden,
remind me that the quantity of the gift is less important than
the quality of the thought that prompted the giving.

Thank You, Lord.

Amen.

Backache Lessons

Some few years ago, I introduced my friend, Pam, to fresh black-eyed peas, and after that she vowed never again to eat dried ones if she could find the fresh variety. Now having moved into a home with enough tillable space for a garden, she was an eager student of my gardening skills.

She had learned of manure, mulch, composting, water, and accumulated salts in the soil. She had also learned of sow bugs, whiteflies, aphids, and shield bugs. She entered her gardening project with all the zeal of a politician seeking office for the first time. The space in her garden was limited, to say the least, but she planted four eight-foot rows of black-eyed peas, along with a whole row of zucchini, broccoli and Brussels sprouts. The peas, alas, turned out to provide an inadequate crop for her family of three. So she picked and froze until she had enough for a meal.

Then, like everything in gardens, the vines died and Pam was distraught. She hadn't enough food in her freezer to take her into the fall months. I counseled her that peas can be planted throughout our growing season here in Las Vegas. Immediately, she re-planted and watched as the peas sprouted and grew, pleased as could be with her handiwork.

On one occasion, I had to go out of state because of a family illness, and asked if she would be so kind as to pick my peas, peppers, tomatoes and anything else ripe that she could find. She agreed, but at the last minute, I did not have to leave. When she came to the appointed task, I told her that she could keep all that we picked anyway, and we set about the gruelling task of pea-picking. Taking three or four "back breaks," we gathered almost a bushel. She was delighted, and spent all the next day shelling and freezing her peas.

Days passed, and one morning she called me, very excited. "Guess what! Guess what! I am so proud of my new peas! I have so many to pick that my back hurt; I had to take two 'back breaks!' That's pretty good, isn't it!"

I had to laugh, because I had never considered the number of "back breaks" criteria for a successful garden. Apparently, there are times the message I think I'm conveying isn't necessarily the one that's being absorbed. But the memory of my friend's enthusiasm for "back breaks" still brings a smile—even when I'm the one out there picking the peas!

Traveling Corn

I have tried many varieties of corn in my garden, and most have given me wonderful ears to savor all year from my freezer. Honey and Pearls, Platinum Lady, Silver Queen, Early Golden, and many others were equally gratifying. Their foliage was beautiful in the garden, providing me and the other creatures there with all manner of benefits.

But I never had corn that actually traveled—until I planted a beautiful variety called "Kandy Korn." The ears were compact, only seven or eight inches long with thirteen or fourteen rows of buttery sweet kernels. The beauty of the eight-foot-tall stalks was in the dark green of the foliage painted with streaks of dark purple on the canes, leaf bases and ear shucks. I so loved looking at them, I resisted cutting the stalks even after I had long since harvested a bumper crop of corn.

One morning as I strolled through the garden, my neighbor, Russ, greeted me over the fence. He admired the lovely corn, commenting on the difference between the Kandy Korn stalks and the shorter, less colorful Golden Early at the other end of the patch.

Since it was nearing Halloween, I asked if he would like some of the stalks for his children's annual front yard display.

"That would be great!" he said. The following Saturday, Russ arrived at our gate with his wheelbarrow, some rope for tying a shock of stalks, and a curved 12-inch scythe.

Setting to his task, he quickly cut and stacked all of the gorgeous stalks, tassels intact, across his barrow. I suggested that he probably had enough for several bundles. He said he didn't know how many he would use, but if he had a surplus, he would just peddle the stalks up and down the street to his neighbors. He knew they would love to have them, because they had spoken often about my beautiful corn.

I had long known that my garden was the gem of the neighborhood, but I didn't realize that one day I might drive through town and see my cornstalks spilling out from other folks' yards.

But then, I shouldn't be surprised. Isn't it logical that a beautiful Halloween variety called "Kandy Korn" would find its way to an appreciative audience? And how often, I mused,

do I mysteriously find my way to just the right person or situation, at just the right time in my life? Once again, I see our Creator's Hand in the process. Certainly, God seems to know at which doorstep the bounty is to be delivered.

Validation

Webster defines "valid" as "being well grounded on facts, evidence. . . having power to be relevant."

I know I want to be relevant in some way, whether as an outstanding parent, the best boss at work, a first-rate partner, or an unforgettable teacher.

I find my validation and relevance from working in my garden. I know that, from bare soil in early spring, I can plant and grow beautiful vegetables and fruit. My garden also brings beauty and serenity into the lives of others. At times, it has even provided solace for troubled spirits and healing for lonely hearts.

Validation for me comes from knowing that, not only can I can provide my family with the best food available anywhere, but I can answer questions when others need help with gardening problems. I may not always know about a specific topic in question, but the answer is given to me when I think of past experiences in my own garden. Validation comes when I am told, "Thank you for helping me solve my problem."

People are unlike any other species on this Earth. Plants and creatures are not in need of continual reassurance that they are relevant. Only people need to be told, "That was a fine dinner," or "What an excellent speech you gave," or "I'm so proud of your school work."

A pat on the back means I am worth something, and I need it as much as food for my body, water for my thirst, or air for me to breathe. And yet, this life-affirming act of validating others takes little time and effort.

Words once spoken cannot be called back, be they good or bad. Therefore, I must try to speak only those words that give support and validation to those who need it. In so doing, I am not only validating others, I am validating myself for recognizing their very special qualities!

Mrs. McFarland's Roses

When I was a young girl, my Grandfather Hicks suffered a massive stroke and was taken to the hospital in town. He lingered there for a week, and because our parents had to stay with him, my younger brother and sister and I were taken into town to stay with our postmistress friend, Mrs. Leary.

We were very sad about Grandfather and, not knowing that he was in a coma, wanted to bring him some flowers to cheer him up. Across the street from Mrs. Leary was a beautiful rose garden belonging to Mrs. McFarland. We couldn't resist crossing the street (with permission) to look at the sweet-smelling rainbow of blossoms.

When Mrs. McFarland came out and asked who we were, we told her, and explained that our Grandfather was in

75

the hospital. "Would you like to take him some of my roses?" she asked, to our almost uncontrollable joy.

Alas, we could not pay for them, but she waved off our objections and began to cut the wonderfully fragrant flowers. Then, she filled the arms of three delighted youngsters. When we presented the blooms to Mrs. Leary, she put them into vases of water, and we went to sleep that night surrounded by the most heavenly fragrance we had ever smelled.

The next day, laden with roses, we went to visit Grandfather. Shyly, we entered the room where the old man lay laboring for breath. We had never been in a hospital room before, and it was an awesome experience for us. The roses were deposited on the bedside table; the room was filled with the heavy scent, and everyone asked us where we had gotten them. We whispered our story and looked at Grandfather to see if he would appreciate them.

Although his face was drawn, his mouth was curled up at one corner under his walrus moustache, and we just knew that we had made him smile. That was one of the fullest moments of my life. Giving roses became, for me, a gesture so rewarding that I still get that same full feeling each time I share a flower or vegetable from my own garden.

Today, when I offer gifts from my own garden, I remember Mrs. McFarland as she loaded roses into the arms of three scrubby little kids. I think I know how she felt, handing a floral rainbow to three children and their Grandfather. God bless you, Mrs. McFarland, wherever you are!

Apples and Love

Somehow, when I think of my father, I think of plain, good-tasting food. When I was a youngster, food was a precious commodity for our family of nine. The sweetest times I can recall were Sunday dinners with all of us sparkling clean in our Sunday best for our guest, the church pastor.

Many years later, and many miles from that time, I visited my father in his Ruidoso, New Mexico home. Here, he had trees galore: apple trees, crabapple trees, cherry trees, and pear trees. Dad was a frugal farmer, and one year, when he had a crop abundance, he built an insulated apple house in his backyard. He then stacked his newspaper-wrapped apples in boxes until they reached the ceiling of the little apple repository. He loved his apples so much, he would stuff two or three of them in his jacket pocket for munching as he worked in the yard. He laughed as he told me, "They are so sweet and juicy, the juice runs off my chin and clear down to my elbows!"

On one special visit, Dad and I went down to the orchard. Although I was forty years old, and my Dad was past seventy with severe angina, we picked apples all weekend. I shinnied up into the trees, the fruit sack around my neck and shoulders. Then, standing precariously on delicate-looking but tough boughs, I leaned, stretched, stooped and pushed my way between the limbs to reach an oh-so-perfect apple.

If I fumbled, I would shout, "Headache!" and Dad, laughing below, would move as quickly as his heart would allow, skillfully avoiding the half-pound missile. Finally, with the fruit sack full, I would inch my way down to the ladder top and unbuckle the sack bottom. Then, Dad would deposit the load into baskets.

I kept a keen eye on him, alert for signs of fatigue, asking when he was slow to rise if he wanted to stop. "No," he would reply each time.

I, from my lofty perch in the treetops, felt just as I had when I was a youngster. I was excited and exhilarated, and felt so very young that weekend working with my father, the scent of apples strong in my nostrils, hair, and clothing. And we worked hard—altogether, we picked thirty bushels of wonderful apples: Rome Beauty, Jonathan, Yellow Delicious, and Winesap.

Back on the ground, I felt the ache in my muscles that reminded me of my true age. But those days were as golden as the Yellow Delicious apples my Dad and I had gathered. I can still hear his delighted chuckle with his favorite comment, "These apples are so sweet and juicy, the juice runs off my chin and clear down to my elbows!"

For me, harvestings are much more than the gathering of fruit and vegetables. They are friendships, family, and wonderful memories. The produce is always satisfying to the taste, but the experience itself is sweet enough to nourish me for a long, long time.

Beauty on Fragile Wings

Years ago, on a cool, fresh morning, I found my thoughts in turmoil. I had a lovely home, a very caring husband, and much to be thankful for. But I felt guilty for not having a job, so I wasn't really able to feel all that thankful.

I had opened our sliding glass doors to the pure, sweet air. Sitting at my table, I observed the lacy fronds of the asparagus waving gently in the phantom breeze. In truth, I was watching for the hummingbird that fed at the nectar hung over my kitchen window.

Suddenly, there he was! The little hummer, wearing an emerald green vest and hood, began feeding hungrily at the bright nectar. Then, as he had a few times before, he moved toward the open door and stopped, suspended on blurred wings. But this time, this time, he entered my kitchen, my earthbound world!

I sat breathless as he flew directly to the painted wind chime hanging on the air conditioner register, touching each tinkling glass panel with his beak. Barely daring to breathe, I moved only my eyes as he darted to the five-globed chandelier directly above me, touching each bright sphere before investigating the spider plant at the bay window. I was captivated by his gracefulness as he explored my world.

The tiny bird then retraced his route back to the chandelier, back to the wind chimes, again touching each brightly painted panel as he had the first time. And then, he darted out the door.

And with the visit from this tiny bird, my world was utterly changed. Earlier, I had been trying to form a prayer of thankfulness, while not quite feeling thankful. Now, thankfulness permeated my entire being. The little hummer had brought me one of the most glorious moments I have ever experienced.

Later, I was able to freely pour out my truly felt gratitude to God for my life, my day, my home, and my visit from beauty on fragile wings.

Changing with the Seasons

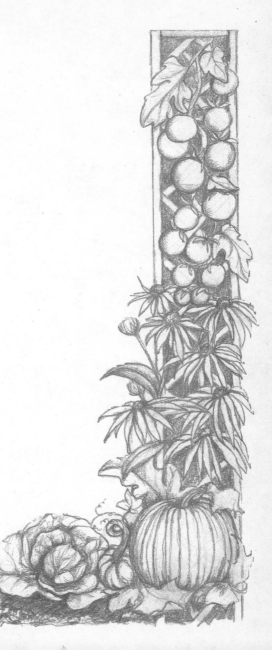

Prayer for Graceful Change

Dear Lord,

In the spring of our lives, we are young and vibrant and as vigorous with life as the tender shoots from the garden bed. We are like the blooms readying to set seed and be prolific.

In summer, we blow in the wind, bending and swaying with the winds and storms like the trees, full and strong. Our lives are as full as lush garden growth and just as productive.

Now, in fall, with aches in our bodies and hearts, we must accept the leaving of loved ones, much as a tree tolerates the loss of its leaves.

And at last, in our winters, we must accept the snow that is falling upon us.

Bless us, Oh Lord, that we may accept the changing seasons of our lives, even as we accept the changing seasons in our gardens.

Thank You, Lord.

Amen.

Fall: A Time for Reflection

Fall is upon us. In a week, it will officially arrive.

This is my favorite time of year because everything takes on a softer image; the weather moderates and the 115-degree days are over. Trees take on softer colors as their leaves go from hard, bright greens to a Technicolor maze of golds, yellows, and reds. Even people seem to take on softer attitudes as they shift away from the trying times of summer vacations, little leagues, out-of-town guests, and school vacation activities.

My garden is entering fall, as well. As the produce slacks off, my house is redolent with spicy vinegar for the sweet pickles. The last of the crop is waiting out the final twelve hours of curing time before getting sealed in sterilized jars for the winter. The black-eyed peas are fewer now, but their size and rich flavor make up for the lack of quantity. The bell peppers are bending to the breaking point with the volume of green and bright red fruit; the carrots are growing crisper and sweeter as they mellow in the earth.

Meanwhile, my desk is growing deeper with students' papers waiting to be graded as the new school term gathers momentum. My evaluations marked in red will let the students know whether or not they are meeting my work criteria. And as I sit and think of meeting criteria, I muse about my life and that of my garden.

Did the garden do its best this year? Could it have been more productive? Did it give what was expected of it? When I wonder about these things, I am reminded that I must look at my own behavior over the past year, and ask those same questions of myself. Did I do my best? Could I have been more productive? Did I do what was expected of me?

I hope I can honestly answer "yes" to all those questions. When I think about it, my garden is nothing more than a reflection of me. It does as I do. If it is tended with care and honesty, it will surpass my expectations. If I express myself in my daily life with care and honesty, I, too, will surpass my expectations.

This does not mean that I will simply perform the chores necessary to keep my own home going; it also means

taking care of those around me. The elderly woman who cannot tolerate the intense summer heat could use a visit from a caring neighbor. My niece could use some encouragement as the world's conflicts threaten to take my nephew off to some distant battlefield. My husband could use some support as he fights daily production quotas and deadlines at work. My students could use a "thumbs up" from me for their efforts. My invalid stepmother halfway across the country could use a call from me to break the monotony of her limited life.

My garden, too, is waiting for my care and attention as the seasons change. Its promise for the fall is great, but it can only return to me what I have put into it. Just as I grade my students on their efforts, so Nature grades my efforts by producing the appropriate quality and quantity of fruits and vegetables.

Will my crops—and I—pass Nature's exam this year? With high hopes and great anticipation, I await the answer in this fall's coming harvest.

Miracle in my Hand

Our cabin in southern Utah had a porch across the front where I had hung two feeders for hummingbirds. Many mornings and evenings I sat there and just marveled at the slyness and cunning of these little birds. The one claiming dominant rights to the feeder would patrol it all day. When he was not feeding, he would perch in the pine tree just around the corner from the feeder, out of sight, but still able to watch for intruders. There have been times when, as the little bird hastily departed the feeding station, he would accidentally crash into the window glass and stun himself. Most of the time, the little hummer would rouse himself and fly away on his own, but once, that was not the case.

It was late summer and Grover and I had just arrived home from a day of trout fishing. We sat on the porch

91

relaxing when two male hummers began duelling over the feeder. The loser, escaping from his attacker, slammed into the window over my head and fell unconscious into a lawn chair at my side. His head was twisted to one side and his tongue protruded through his tiny beak. His feet were twitching convulsively as he lay on his back.

Dismayed, I picked him up and lay him on his back in the palm of my hand. I tried to revive him by pumping his legs and rubbing his stomach, but there was no response.

"I'm afraid he's dead," I told Grover, who was watching with concern.

"He'll be all right, he's just knocked out," my husband assured me.

I turned the bird over on his stomach and straightened his head, but he remained unresponsive. Then, I began to lightly rub him from the base of his beak to his tail, trying to rouse him.

All at once, his head began to wobble from side to side! After a few seconds, he actually raised his head, pushed himself up, and flew off unsteadily. But he didn't get too far, alighting on the fence a few feet away.

"I'm afraid something will get him!" I cried in alarm. "Look at him, he's still addled. I wonder if I can catch him."

I started toward the little hummer, but when I was about four feet away, he flew toward the other side of the yard, once again landing on the fence near the ground.

Purposefully, I continued my approach; I was relieved that, as I got closer, he continued to sit, bobbing his head from side to side.

I squatted down in front of the bird, hoping he wouldn't try to fly away, but I needn't have worried; he just sat, dazed, on the fence.

Tentatively, I extended my finger to the top of his head and stroked it several times. Encouraged by his lack of reaction, I stroked him under his beak and down his breast. Amazingly, he just sat there, his little head still bobbing.

"Grover," I called. "How often have you seen someone petting a hummingbird that's sitting on a fence?"

"Not very often," he replied, grinning.

"Do you think anyone will believe this?" I asked.

"I see it and I can hardly believe it!" Grover laughed.

Suddenly, the little bird stopped bobbing his head, looked directly at me for five seconds or so, and flew straight up and out of sight.

Somehow, I knew he would be all right, and *I* felt wonderful! On this day, God had allowed me to hold a miracle in my hand.

C h a n g e s

As I sit on my patio, I am once again listening to my garden. Instead of a pale blue summer sky above, a gray canopy of clouds hangs heavy with impending showers. Everything is quiet—even the mockingbird, who is usually noisily challenging all contenders to his feeding rights to the giant sunflower. This state of affairs is most unusual.

I noticed a change in air temperature first. This past Monday morning, the temperature reached a high of 103 degrees; next day, it topped out at 98. This did not surprise me, since this is September; what I hadn't expected was the evening and night temperatures falling to below 60 degrees! Already, my garden is beginning to react to the changes in the soil that herald cooler weather.

The leaves of the berry vines are showing reddish tinges and the black-eyed peas are turning a golden yellow;

now that their thermostats are turned off, an early demise approaches. And, in spite of daily overhead irrigation, the cornstalks rustle in the breezes like crumpled dry paper blowing across a courtyard.

The potatoes are ready to be dug up. The peas will soon be history. The limas are still going strong, and will continue to, until frost. The leeks and carrots have been hilled up for a long winter's nap.

My garden's animal life is changing, as well. Soon there will be no hummingbirds and no little red finches. But there will be a multitude of mourning doves, blackbirds, and sparrows, all intent on the seeds left in my garden after harvest. The kestrals have long since found more suitable weather, leaving my number one adversary, the chipmunks, to do what they will.

Today, in fact, I watched Mama Chipmunk introduce her new brood to the garden and all its goodies. There they were, Mama with four or five baby chippies nursing atop the pilaster in the middle of the back fence. The mockingbird noticed them, too, and went over for a closer look. Mama and most of the little ones ducked into the pilaster, but one baby chippie hightailed it around the corner, posthaste! The mockingbird eventually drove them all away, his raucus voice and persistence too fervent for them to ignore.

Now winter Swiss chard, turnips, lettuce, cabbage, broccoli, beets, radishes and spinach are just peeking over the

furrows, a delicious potential meal for the chipmunks. I know these hungry little rodents will soon be munching away at my vegetables, if they haven't already begun.

Even my kitchen reflects the forthcoming change in season. Gone are the light stir-fried and steamed vegetables; gone are the melon dinners, salad lunches, freshly picked sweet peas eaten raw. Instead, there is a heady aroma of short ribs slowly baking with onions, carrots and potatoes. A nice pot of limas with diced ham simmers on the back burner, and roasted corn on the cob from the freezer nestles against a juicy T-bone steak on the outdoor grill.

I hear the mournful sound of the wind outside my door, and am strangely comforted. It reminds me how lucky I was to see the tiny hummingbird chasing the mockingbird out of the corn; how fascinating it was to watch a chipmunk play tag along the fence with a big, fat, brown lizard; how inspiring it was to observe the male kestral feeding his mate. And even though chippies are the scourge of my garden, how fortunate I was to witness baby chipmunks nursing at their mother's belly!

I listen to the wind carefully, hearing its recital of my garden's wonders. And I know that, if I am to hear its wonderful secrets, I must be very still—both inside and out.

A Garden of Friends

Yesterday, I pulled the dead and dying squash vines from the garden. They had given me a bumper crop of tender, sweet zucchini this year, but their time was past. Hanging on tenuously are the spaghetti and butternut squash, filling the spaces left by the vacated zucchini.

The green beans are feeling the effects of the cooling earth beneath them, and are nearly finished with their short, abundant season. Each time I go to my kitchen door, the asparagus greets me with lacy green fronds polka-dotted with red berries. I hate to see the season end; it's been so rich, bringing me and mine an abundance of food as well as birds and butterflies. My garden has been a joy to observe all year long.

My plants have flourished in the garden, and the tunneling activities of the insects have helped propagate the plants by aerating and refining the soil.

And what can I say of the birds? All year they have fed, played, mated and bathed in my garden while serenading me, not only with their songs, but with a show of color rich enough to please the eyes of the greatest monarch.

I wonder, as I look at the passing seasons, at the procession of friends and acquaintances through my life. Where are they now? Like the seasons in my garden, they have made my life richer during their time. They fed me when I sought spiritual and emotional nourishment, as I did them. And each had a season in my life's garden.

As with all things in my garden, I thank God for their time and season there. Without them, I would not have become the person I am. It is sad to look upon present friends and acquaintances, knowing that they, too, will someday leave my life. But knowing that, through them, I become a better and more understanding person, I can accept their departures.

So I do not weep for my dead and dying garden, nor for the cycling of friends; I celebrate them all with anticipation of even richer times ahead, and cherish now the time we have together.

Dorothy

Last evening, I visited my neighbors, Jack and Dorothy; they live just across the backyard fence. Not having fully developed their own garden yet, they check daily on mine with a proprietary concern. At least once a week, I take them a bag of fresh produce; they call me their "own private bag lady."

This has been, perhaps, one of the most enjoyable summers I have ever spent. Jack and Dorothy's obvious enjoyment of my garden's vegetables and flowers has warmed me with delight.

But yesterday, I heard chilling news—the doctor's report on Dorothy's condition: terminal.

"I'm not going to make it," she told me, tears filling her eyes. "You tell her, Jack, I can't."

Her cancer was accelerating, and her weakening condition was quite visible to my untrained eyes. We knew

that she had cancer, but believed it was in remission. I was stunned, speechless. Holding her cold hands in mine, I thought back to just a week before when Jack and Dorothy had visited our cabin for a few days.

As she prepared for the trip, Dorothy had remarked, "There are three things I want to do this year: go fishing again on Blue Mesa, celebrate our fortieth anniversary, and see John married." It had become obvious that she could not make the fishing trip to Colorado, so we invited the couple to come fishing with us in southwestern Utah.

That week, Dorothy sat in the bow of our small boat, gazing out across the rough desert mountains with a wonderful smile on her face. The weather was disappointing; it was rainy, cold and blustery, making the water choppy and very unpleasant. I, myself, was miserably cold and uncomfortable, but Dorothy was ecstatic.

"Isn't this just beautiful? How can anyone not believe in God when they see this?" She hooked a nice little trout, and lurched forward weakly to pull him in. She was elated with her catch and next day, caught another one! This time, however, Jack had to help her bring the small fish in.

Later that day, we returned to the cabin. The men decided to go to a smaller nearby reservoir and continue fishing. Dorothy and I sat on the cabin porch and watched hummingbirds battle for sipping rights at the feeder. We talked for hours in the easy, uncomplicated way friends do when there are no barriers between them.

We spoke of the joys we each had been given, and the great sadnesses we had experienced. The time was pure gold. If I never have another enjoyable day at our cabin, I will forever thank God that Dorothy and I had that one.

Now I must face the fact that Dorothy will not be watching over my garden much longer. When we returned home, she told me that she wished she could walk among the plants in my garden and see them up close.

She had never seen broccoli growing; mine were lush. Resting frequently to catch her breath, she walked slowly, examining each vegetable, while Jack and I held her hands to support her. Dorothy told me that when she stepped up on the concrete blocks Jack had placed for her in their yard to look over my fence, she felt that "I'm looking over the fence at Paradise."

Each garden I have created has had a special reason for being. Some have produced ripe, luscious fruit; others have produced crisp, healthy vegetables. But the season of this particular garden was for Dorothy.

Dorothy brought to me a wonderful, memorable friendship I will always cherish. She added richness to my life that I will never forget. She and Jack were like the warm sunshine that makes the garden of my soul grow and flourish.

I don't know what the future will bring for me as I continue to tend my garden. But I do know that I will never again plant a garden without thinking of Dorothy climbing up on her concrete blocks, eager to "look over the fence at Paradise."

Fence Corners and Life

It may seem strange that fence corners would have anything at all to do with life, much less with love, caring or family. However, sometimes mundane things such as fence corners have everything to do with these.

Adjacent to the farm where I spent my first fourteen years lived a family, the Dean Brumleys. They were very good friends who helped us survive those lean Depression years. Any time our well failed, they provided access to their water. When our money was short, they hired me and my siblings to pick cotton, head maize, clean house or do laundry and ironing. They were an important part of my childhood, always there.

Although we lived thirteen miles outside of town on a dusty, dry, caliche farm, some of my fondest memories

center on that place and time. We children could wander anywhere, miles from home, and know just by looking at the fence corners where we were, how far we were from home, and which way to go back. There was a real sense of safety in knowing our boundaries, our fence corners.

However, like many country children, I couldn't wait to get away from our farm, and in time, I married and moved away.

Later, the marriage failed. I was devastated and very alone, or so it seemed, looking for safety and a sense of belonging. My search took me, through a position at Western Texas College, back to my home town, back to within thirteen miles of the farm where I had grown up. But, although "home" again, I felt like a stranger; outside of a few people with whom I had attended grade school eons ago, I knew no one.

One project that had kept me going was a small volume of poetry I had written, dealing not only with the trauma, sadness, and defeat of a failed relationship, but also the joy and hope of succeeding in a new environment. Now, I was struggling to find a title for this work.

It was the late seventies, when independence and equality for women were buzzwords. I considered naming the little book something like, "From the Heart of a Woman," "The Soul of a Woman," or "Liberated Woman." But I didn't really feel liberated; I just felt alone.

One Sunday afternoon, I impulsively drove out to see our old homesite. As I drove over the small hill just above the farmhouse, I caught my breath. The hill wasn't as large as I'd remembered it. My grandfather's house and orchard were gone. But my desire to go back home was so strong, I could almost feel it physically. Where was the windmill tower? What had happened to the mesquite trees where my younger brother and sister and I had played for hours? The corn patches, Sudan fields, cotton and maize fields had all reverted to native grass, and five oil well pumps marked the four corners of our farmsite.

I drove slowly down the hill, passed the sand bed, turned into the gate and followed the gravel-topped road to the top of the hill, where I parked and sat very quietly for a very long time. Once again, I could hear my younger brother, sister and me laughing together. I could hear Mother calling us to do our chores and come to dinner. I could hear the growling tornados moving toward our house and our frightened screams as we hurried to gather in the young turkeys and chickens before the hail started. I could almost smell the odors one remembers most strongly about their childhood: the pungent livestock odor, newly chopped hay, frying sausages.

Then, it was gone. I cried. I sobbed for all the hurts, the disappointments, wrong choices, and other real or imagined trials of my life.

Finally, my red eyes dried, I started back to town. As I rounded the corner and drove down the road by the Brumley's, I mused, "I think I'll drive up Brumley's Lane. It's been thirty-five years since I was there."

Turning the corner up the lane, I saw a fence corner surrounded with black-eyed Susans. I stopped cold in my tracks. Now I had my book cover. Now I had my title. The cover would feature a drawing of Brumley's fence corner, and the title would be "Bittersweet Autumn." I got out of my car and took several Polaroid shots of the corner and drove, exhausted but content, back to town, back to reality.

Since that day, fence corners have reminded me of belonging, security, safety, comfort, stability, and love. Fence corners, in whatever form they may take, are the anchors in my life. I thank God for providing these indicators of where I have been, where I am now, and where I am going.

My Personal Reflections

My Personal Reflections

My Personal Reflections

My Personal Reflections